LAUGH
-Out-
LOUD
JOLLY
JOKES for KIDS

2-IN-1 COLLECTION OF CHRISTMAS JOKES AND ADVENTURE JOKES

LAUGH
-Out-
LOUD
JoLLy

JOKES
for KIDS

ROB ELLIOTT

HARPER
An Imprint of HarperCollinsPublishers

Library of Congress Control Number: 2019944326
ISBN 978-0-06-288808-2

   21 22 23   LSC   10 9 8 7 6 5 4 3

First Edition

LAUGH
-Out-
LOUD
CHRISTMAS
JOKES
for KIDS

To my mother, Maribeth, and my dad, Robert (1937–2012): You gave me a deep love for the holidays and taught me the true meaning of Christmas.

With all my heart,

Rob

Q: **What did the Christmas tree say to the ornament?**

A: "Quit hanging around."

Q: **What do snowmen eat for lunch?**

A: Brrrr-itos

Q: **Where does Santa keep his money?**

A: In a snowbank

Q: **What is a Christmas tree's least favorite month of the year?**

A: Sep-timber

Q: What do you get when you mix a dog with a snowflake?

A: Frostbite

Q: Why did Santa feel bad about himself?

A: Because he had low elf-esteem.

Q: Why don't lobsters give Christmas presents?

A: Because they're shellfish.

Q: What do you call a cat who gives you presents?

A: Santa Paws

Q: What did Frosty wear to the wedding?

A: His snowsuit

Q: What is Jack Frost's favorite movie?

A: *The Blizzard of Oz*

Knock, knock.

Who's there?

Peas.

Peas who?

Peas tell me what you're giving me

for Christmas!

Knock, knock.

Who's there?

Norway.

Norway who?

There is Norway I'm kissing anybody

under the mistletoe!

Q: What is the coldest month of the year?

A: Decemb-rrrrr

Q: What is a tiger's favorite Christmas song?

A: "Jungle Bells"

Q: Why was Santa dressed up?

A: Because he was going to the snowball.

Q: Why do snowmen always change their minds?

A: Because they're flaky!

Q: Where do elves go to vote?

A: The North Poll

Q: Where does the Easter Bunny get his eggs at Christmastime?

A: From the three French hens

Q: What does Santa give Rudolph when he has bad breath?

A: Orna-mints

Q: What do snowmen wear on their feet?

A: Snowshoes

Knock, knock.

Who's there?

Freeze.

Freeze who?

Freeze a Jolly Good Fellow.

Q: Who brings Christmas presents to a shark?

A: Santa Jaws

Q: What's a polar bear's favorite cereal?

A: Ice Krispies

Knock, knock.

Who's there?

Hugo.

Hugo who?

Hugo sit on Santa's lap first, then I'll go second.

Knock, knock.

Who's there?

Dubai.

Dubai who?

I'm off Dubai some Christmas presents for you!

Knock, knock.

Who's there?

Butter.

Butter who?

You butter watch out. You butter not cry. You butter not pout I'm telling you why. . . .

Knock, knock.

Who's there?

Elf.

Elf who?

Elf finish wrapping the presents right away!

Q: What always falls at Christmas but never gets hurt?

A: Snow!

Santa: Elf, I have something to tell you.

Elf: I'm all ears.

Q: Why does Rudolph's nose shine at night?

A: Because he's a light sleeper.

Q: **What did the gingerbread man do when he sprained his ankle?**

A: He iced it.

Q: **What do elves post on Facebook?**

A: Elf-ies

Q: **What do gingerbread men do before they go to bed?**

A: Change their cookie sheets

Q: **How do frogs celebrate Christmas?**

A: They kiss under the mistle-toad.

Q: **How do snowmen carry their books to school?**

A: In their snowpacks

Q: **What do grumpy sheep say during the holidays?**

A: "Baa, baa, humbug."

Q: **What is a sheep's favorite Christmas song?**

A: "Fleece Navidad"

Knock, knock.

Who's there?

Canoe.

Canoe who?

Canoe help me put up the Christmas tree?

Knock, knock.

Who's there?

Wooden shoe.

Wooden shoe who?

Wooden shoe like to know what you're getting for Christmas?

Knock, knock.

Who's there?

Waldo.

Waldo who?

Waldo we do to celebrate New Year's Eve?

Q: Why do elves go to school?

A: To learn the elf-abet

- -

Q: Why can't a Christmas tree learn to knit?

A: Because they always drop their needles.

Q: Why doesn't Santa let the elves use his computer?

A: They always delete the Christmas cookies.

Q: What is Santa's favorite kind of sandwich?

A: Peanut butter and jolly

Q: What is a penguin's favorite kind of cereal?

A: Frosted Flakes

Q: Where do Santa's reindeer stop for coffee?

A: Star-bucks

Knock, knock.

Who's there?

Myrrh.

Myrrh who?

Myrrh Christmas and a Happy New Year!

Knock, knock.

Who's there?

Udder.

Udder who?

Udder the tree you'll find your present!

Q: What do fish sing at Christmastime?

A: Christmas corals

Q: What do ducks like to eat at

   Christmas parties?

A: Cheese and quackers

Knock, knock.

   Who's there?

Ya.

   Ya who?

Wow, ya really excited about Christmas!

Knock, knock.

   Who's there?

Iva.

   Iva who?

Iva bunch of decorations to put on the tree.

Knock, knock.

Who's there?

Avenue.

Avenue who?

Avenue started your Christmas shopping yet?

Knock, knock.

Who's there?

Cannoli.

Cannoli who?

I cannoli eat one more Christmas cookie!

Q: Why did Santa pay top dollar for a box of candy canes?

A: Because they were in MINT condition!

Q: What goes *ho, ho, ho, thump*?

A: Santa laughing his head off!

Q: **What do you call a snowman who vacations in Florida?**

A: A puddle

Knock, knock.

Who's there?

Snow.

Snow who?

I snow what Santa's bringing you for Christmas.

Knock, knock.

Who's there?

Snowman.

Snowman who?

Snowman has ever seen Santa's workshop at the North Pole.

Q: **What do you get when you cross a pinecone and a polar bear?**

A: A fur tree

Q: **Why did the math teacher get sick after Christmas dinner?**

A: He had too much pi.

Q: **What is an elf's favorite part of school?**

A: Snow-and-tell

Q: **What do you get when you combine a Christmas tree and an iPod?**

A: A pineapple

Knock, knock.

Who's there?

Whale.

Whale who?

Whale, I can't believe the holidays are almost here!

Q: What does an elf listen to on the radio?

A: Wrap music

Q: Why doesn't Santa hide presents in the closet?

A: He has Claus-trophobia.

Knock, knock.

Who's there?

Dexter.

Dexter who?

Dexter halls with boughs of holly!

Q: How do snowmen spend their

Christmas vacations?

A: Chilling out

Knock, knock.

Who's there?

Arthur.

Arthur who?

Arthur any more Christmas presents to open?

Q: What does Santa give his reindeer for a stomachache?

A: Elk-a-Seltzer

Q: What do gingerbread men use when they break their legs?

A: Candy canes

Q: What is green, white, and red all over?

A: An elf with sunburn

Q: Why didn't the rope get any presents?

A: Because it was knotty.

Q: What did Mrs. Claus say to Rudolph when he was grumpy?

A: "You need to lighten up!"

Q: **How much did Santa pay for his reindeer?**

A: A few bucks

Q: **Why did the gingerbread man go to the doctor?**

A: He was feeling crumb-y!

Q: **What is something you can throw during the holidays but never catch?**

A: A Christmas party

Q: **Why doesn't Santa ever have spare change?**

A: Because he's Jolly Old St. Nickel-less.

Q: **How does a polar bear write out his Christmas list?**

A: With a pen-guin

Q: **Why was the cat put on Santa's naughty list?**

A: Because he was a cheat-ah.

Q: **How did the orange get into the Christmas stocking?**

A: It squeezed its way in!

Knock, knock.

Who's there?

Annie.

Annie who?

Annie-body want some Christmas cookies?

Q: **Why was the cat afraid to climb the Christmas tree?**

A: It was scared of the bark!

Q: Why did Santa carry a giant sponge while delivering presents in Florida?

A: He wanted to soak up the sun!

Q: Why did Santa have a clock in his sleigh?

A: He wanted to watch time fly.

Q: How did the pony break its Christmas present?

A: It wouldn't stop horsing around.

Q: Why did the baker give everybody free cookies for Christmas?

A: Because he had a lot of dough!

Knock, knock.

Who's there?

Donut.

Donut who?

I donut know how Santa gets down the chimney on Christmas Eve!

Knock, knock.

Who's there?

Justin.

Justin who?

You're Justin time for Christmas carols.

Knock, knock.

Who's there?

Willie.

Willie who?

Willie keep his New Year's resolution this year?

31

Knock, knock.

Who's there?

Oldest.

Oldest who?

Oldest Christmas shopping is giving me a headache!

Knock, knock.

Who's there?

Snow place.

Snow place who?

There's snow place like home.

Q: What does the Easter Bunny like to drink during the holidays?

A: Eggnog

Knock, knock.

Who's there?

Nutella.

Nutella who?

There's Nutella what Santa might bring for Christmas this year.

Rita: What time is it when a polar bear sits in your chair?

Adam: I'm not sure.

Rita: It's time to get a new chair.

Knock, knock.

Who's there?

Water.

Water who?

Water you doing for New Year's Eve?

Q: Why is Santa so good at gardening?

A: Because he likes to hoe, hoe, hoe.

Knock, knock.

Who's there?

Tibet.

Tibet who?

Go Tibet early tonight, because Santa is coming!

Q: What did the astronaut get for Christmas?

A: A launch box

Q: What is a skunk's favorite Christmas song?

A: "Jingle Smells"

- -

Knock, knock.

Who's there?

Juicy.

Juicy who?

Juicy all the pretty Christmas lights?

Knock, knock.

Who's there?

Rabbit.

Rabbit who?

Rabbit up with paper and ribbon, and put it under the tree.

Q: What kind of motorcycle does Santa drive?

A: A Holly Davidson

Knock, knock.

Who's there?

Quiche.

Quiche who?

Quiche me under the mistletoe!

Knock, knock.

Who's there?

Jester.

Jester who?

In jester minute it'll be the New Year!

Q: What's a mermaid's favorite Christmas story?

A: *A Christmas Coral*

Q: **What did the rattlesnakes do at their Christmas party?**

A: They hissed under the mistletoe.

Q: **What do elves use to wash their hands?**

A: Santa-tizer

Q: **What do you call it when people are afraid of Santa?**

A: Claus-trophobic

Q: **What do boxers like to drink at Christmas parties?**

A: Punch!

Knock, knock.

Who's there?

Yule.

Yule who?

Yule really like your Christmas present this year.

Knock, knock.

Who's there?

Anna.

Anna who?

Anna partridge in a pear tree.

Q: How did the crab wish his mom a Merry Christmas?

A: He called her on his shell phone.

Q: **Why does a cat take so long to wrap Christmas presents?**

A: He won't stop until they're purr-fect.

Q: **Why did Santa go buy more reindeer?**

A: They were on sale and didn't cost much doe!

Q: **Why did the elf have to stay after school?**

A: He was in trouble for losing his gnome-work.

Knock, knock.

Who's there?

Roach.

Roach who?

I roach you a letter to wish you Merry Christmas!

Q: How does Frosty get around?

A: On his ice-cycle

Q: What do pigs use to write their Christmas list for Santa?

A: A pig pen

Q: How do elves learn to chop down a Christmas tree?

A: They go to boarding school.

Q: Why did the Christmas tree go to bed early?

A: It was bushed!

Q: What does Frosty do when he feels stressed out?

A: He takes a chill pill.

Q: Why was the chicken put on Santa's naughty list?

A: It kept laying deviled eggs.

Q: What do you get when you cross a lobster and Santa?

A: Santa Claws

Knock, knock.

Who's there?

Arthur.

Arthur who?

My Arthur-ritis is acting up from the winter weather.

Q: What is Santa's favorite singer?

A: Elf-is Presley

Knock, knock.

Who's there?

Wart.

Wart who?

Wart is your favorite Christmas carol?

Q: What do you call a snowman's kids?

A: Chilled-ren

Q: What did the one penguin say to the other?

A: "Ice to meet you."

Q: What's a dinosaur's least favorite reindeer?

A: Comet

Q: What do polar bears wear on their heads?

A: Snowcaps

Q: **What do penguins use in science class?**

A: Beak-ers

Q: **What did the candy cane say to the ornament?**

A: "Hang in there."

Q: **What do you call it when the elves take a break?**

A: A Santa pause

George: Whose music is best for decking the halls?

James: A-wreath-a Franklin's!

Q: How does the alphabet change during the holidays?

A: The Christmas alphabet has noel.

Knock, knock.

Who's there?

Owl.

Owl who?

Owl always love to celebrate Christmas.

Q: What is Santa Claus's nationality?

A: North Polish

Knock, knock.

Who's there?

Alba.

Alba who?

Alba home for Christmas.

Knock, knock.

Who's there?

Wayne.

Wayne who?

A Wayne a manger.

Josh: Do you know how much Santa paid for his sleigh and reindeer?

Jeff: Maybe a few bucks?

Josh: Nothing! It was on the house.

Q: What do you call a polar bear in the Caribbean?

A: Lost!

Q: What did the chicken have to do after eating all the Christmas cookies?

A: Egg-cercise

Knock, knock.

Who's there?

Uno.

Uno who?

Uno Christmas is a season for giving.

Knock, knock.

Who's there?

Latte.

Latte who?

Thanks a latte for all the Christmas presents!

Q: What kind of cookies make Santa laugh?

A: Snickerdoodles

Q: Why wouldn't Rudolph stay in the barn?

A: Because he was un-stable.

Q: What's an elf's favorite Christmas song?

A: "I'll Be Gnome for Christmas"

Q: What does a whale write in his Christmas cards?

A: Sea-sons greetings!

Knock, knock.

Who's there?

Turnip.

Turnip who?

Turnip the Christmas music!

Q: What does Santa wear when he goes golfing?

A: A tee-shirt

Knock, knock.

Who's there?

Dishes.

Dishes who?

Dishes going to be the best Christmas we've ever had.

Q: How did the turtle behave at the Christmas party?

A: He wouldn't come out of his shell.

- -

Knock, knock.

Who's there?

Interrupting Santa.

Interrupting San—

Ho, ho, ho!

Q: How do you know Santa is good at karate?

A: Because he wears a black belt.

Knock, knock.

Who's there?

Pasture.

Pasture who?

Pasture eggnog—I'm thirsty!

Q: Which one of Santa's reindeer likes to clean the workshop?

A: Comet

Q: How did Santa feel when his reindeer got fleas?

A: It really ticked him off!

Q: What do you have in December that's not in any other month?

A: The letter *D*

Q: What's a mime's favorite Christmas carol?

A: "Silent Night"

Q: What do snowmen say when they play hide-and-seek?

A: "I-cy you!"

Q: What do polar bears put on their tacos?

A: Chilly sauce

Q: Why does Santa go down the chimney?

A: Because it soots him.

Q: Why does a broken drum make a great Christmas present?

A: Because you just can't beat it!

Q: Who does Frosty like to visit during the holidays?

A: His aunt Arctica

Q: What's a polar bear's favorite dinner?

A: Ham-brrrrr-gers

Tongue Twisters

Crispy Christmas cookies

Twelve twisted elves

Santa's snowy sleigh

Plump penguins

Q: Where do skunks like to sit during Christmas church service?

A: In the front pew

Q: What do you get when you cross a dinosaur and an evergreen?

A: A tree rex

Q: Why were Santa's reindeer so itchy?

A: From the antarc-ticks

Knock, knock.

Who's there?

Watson.

Watson who?

Watson your Christmas wish list this year?

Knock, knock.

Who's there?

Yoda.

Yoda who?

Yoda one I want to wish a Merry Christmas!

Knock, knock.

Who's there?

Soda.

Soda who?

It's soda-pressing that the holidays are almost over!

Q: What did one iceberg say to the other?

A: "I think we're drifting apart."

Knock, knock.

Who's there?

Ivy.

Ivy who?

Ivy lot of Christmas cards to put in the mail!

Q: How do snowmen like their root beer?

A: In a frosted mug

Q: What did the basil say to the oregano?

A: "Seasoning's greetings."

Q: Why couldn't Jack Frost go

Christmas shopping?

A: Because his bank account was frozen!

- -

Sam: Did you have fun at the pig's Christmas party?

Sue: No, it was a boar.

Knock, knock.

Who's there?

Brett.

Brett who?

I Brett you don't know what's in your Christmas stocking!

Q: What do you get when you cross Santa Claus and the Easter Bunny?

A: Jolly beans

Q: How did Humpty Dumpty feel after he finished Christmas shopping?

A: Eggs-hausted

Q: Why did Rudolph put his money in the freezer?

A: He wanted some cold, hard cash!

Q: Where do crocodiles keep their eggnog?

A: In the refriger-gator

Knock, knock.

Who's there?

Otter.

Otter who?

You otter come to my house for Christmas this year.

Q: Why was the owl so popular at the Christmas party?

A: He was a hoot!

Q: How do reindeer carry their oats?

A: In a buck-et

Knock, knock.

Who's there?

Nacho.

Nacho who?

It's nacho turn to open a Christmas present.

Q: Why won't snowmen eat any carrot cake?

A: They're afraid it has boogers in it.

Q: What do you get when you combine Santa Claus and Sherlock Holmes?

A: Santa Clues

Q: How do Santa's reindeer know when it's time to deliver presents?

A: They check their calen-deer.

Q: Why do fishermen send Santa so many letters?

A: They love dropping him a line.

Knock, knock.

Who's there?

Bacon.

Bacon who?

I'm bacon dozens of Christmas cookies this year!

Q: Why didn't the beetle like Christmas?

A: Because he was a humbug.

Q: What is Santa's favorite kind of candy?

A: Jolly Ranchers

Q: Why did Frosty get kicked out of the farmer's market?

A: He was caught picking his nose.

Q: Why wouldn't the turkey eat dessert after Christmas dinner?

A: He was too stuffed.

Q: Where do bugs like to shop for their Christmas presents?

A: At the flea market

Q: Why doesn't Santa ever worry about the past?

A: Because he's always focused on the present.

Q: What's the best state for listening to Christmas music?

A: South Carol-ina

Q: What kind of animal needs an umbrella?

A: Rain-deer

Q: What happened when Santa took a nap in the fireplace?

A: He slept like a log.

Knock, knock.

Who's there?

Acid.

Acid who?

Acid I'd stop by and bring you a

Christmas present.

Q: What do you call decorations hanging from

Rudolph's antlers?

A: Christmas horn-aments

Q: Why did the snowman's mouth hurt?

A: Because he had a coal sore.

Q: What do polar bears eat for lunch?

A: Iceberg-ers

Knock, knock.

Who's there?

Walnut.

Walnut who?

I walnut let the holidays go by without wishing you a Merry Christmas!

Knock, knock.

Who's there?

Muffin.

Muffin who?

Naughty kids get muffin for Christmas.

Q: Where do people sing Christmas songs quietly?

A: Bethle-hum

Q: How do you find your way to the New Year's Eve party?

A: Follow the auld lang signs.

Knock, knock.

Who's there?

Les.

Les who?

Les go caroling and get some hot chocolate!

Q: What happened when the dentist didn't get a Christmas present?

A: It really hurt his fillings.

Knock, knock.

Who's there?

Mustache.

Mustache who?

I mustache you to come to my Christmas party!

Q: What do you get when you combine a penguin and a jalapeño?

A: A chilly pepper

Knock, knock.

Who's there?

Meow.

Meow who?

Meow-y Christmas!

Q: How do you decorate a scientist's lab for Christmas?

A: With a chemis-tree

Knock, knock.

Who's there?

Dachshund.

Dachshund who?

Dachshund through the snow in a one-horse open sleigh.

Q: What shoes did the baker wear while baking holiday bread?

A: His loafers

Q: What kinds of trees wear gloves in the winter?

A: Palm trees

Q: Why don't you want to make a snowman angry?

A: He might have a total meltdown.

Knock, knock.

Who's there?

Dragon.

Dragon who?

I'm dragon my feet on getting my Christmas shopping done.

Q: Who watched out for the snowman during the blizzard?

A: His snow angel

Q: Why did the mom put her son in the corner after he went snowboarding?

A: She wanted him to warm up in 90 degrees.

Knock, knock.

Who's there?

Cole.

Cole who?

Cole goes in naughty kids' stockings.

Q: Why would you invite a mushroom to a Christmas party?

A: Because he's a fungi.

Q: What do you call a dentist who cleans the abominable snowman's teeth?

A: CRAZY!!!

Q: What do Halloween mummies and Christmas elves have in common?

A: They both have a lot of wrapping.

Q: What kind of drink is never ready on time?

A: Hot choco-late

Knock, knock.

Who's there?

Butcher.

Butcher who?

Butcher arms around me and give me a kiss

under the mistletoe.

Q: Why don't polar bears and penguins

get along?

A: Because they're polar opposites.

Q: What do you call a cow that lives in an igloo?

A: An Eski-moo

Q: What do you call Frosty's cell phone?

A: A snow-mobile

Q: What do you give a baboon for Christmas?

A: A monkey wrench

Q: What do you give a wasp for Christmas?

A: A bee-bee gun

Q: What do squirrels have for breakfast on Christmas morning?

A: Do-nuts

Q: **What did the whale get in its Christmas stocking?**

A: Blubber gum

Q: **What do you get when Jack Frost turns on the radio?**

A: Really cool music

Q: **Why didn't the cow like its crummy Christmas present?**

A: It was a milk dud.

Q: **How do starfish celebrate the holiday season?**

A: With yule-tide greetings

- -

Knock, knock.

Who's there?

Hailey.

Hailey who?

I'm Hailey a cab so we'll make it to the Christmas party on time!

Q: What do you give a lamb for Christmas?

A: A sheeping bag

Knock, knock.

Who's there?

Howie.

Howie who?

Howie going to get that big star on top of the Christmas tree?

Knock, knock.

Who's there?

Noah.

Noah who?

Noah good place to buy candy canes?

Knock, knock.

Who's there?

Taco.

Taco who?

Let's taco 'bout what we'll do for

Christmas vacation!

- -

Knock, knock.

Who's there?

Dawn.

Dawn who?

Dawn forget to leave cookies for Santa on

Christmas Eve!

Knock, knock.

Who's there?

Betty.

Betty who?

I Betty can't guess what I got him for Christmas!

Knock, knock.

Who's there?

Cold.

Cold who?

Cold you come out and build a snowman

with me?

73

Q: What happened to Santa when he went down the chimney?

A: He got the flue.

Q: What do you get from a cow that receives too many presents for Christmas?

A: Spoiled milk!

Knock, knock.

Who's there?

Luke.

Luke who?

Luke up in the sky for Santa's sleigh!

Knock, knock.

Who's there?

Howard.

Howard who?

Howard you like to make some Christmas cookies?

Q: How did the mad scientist cause a blizzard?

A: He was brainstorming.

Jimmy: What do you call a wreath under a pile of snow?

Joey: A holly bury

Q: Why did the librarian have to miss the Christmas party?

A: She was double-booked.

Q: Why did the polar bear get glasses?

A: To improve its ice-sight (eyesight)

Q: How does an Eskimo fix his broken sled?

A: With i-glue

Q: Why did Santa sing lullabies to his sack?

A: He wanted a sleeping bag.

Q: Why did Rudolph need braces?

A: Because he had buck teeth.

Q: Why did Santa use Rudolph to guide his sleigh?

A: It was a bright idea.

Q: What did one Christmas light say to the other?

A: "Do you want to go out tonight?"

Q: Why was Mrs. Claus crying?

A: She stubbed her mistletoe.

Q: Why is the Grinch so good at gardening?

A: He has a green thumb.

Q: Why was the frosting so stressed out?

A: It was spread too thin.

Q: **Why wouldn't the parakeet buy his girlfriend a Christmas present?**

A: Because he was cheep.

Q: **Why are pigs so fun at Christmas parties?**

A: Because they go hog wild.

Q: **What do you call a guy whose snowmobile breaks down?**

A: A cab

Q: **Why don't you invite the Polar Express to dinner?**

A: It always choo-choos with its mouth open.

Knock, knock.

Who's there?

Raymond.

Raymond who?

Raymond me to leave out some cookies

for Santa.

Knock, knock.

Who's there?

Johanna.

Johanna who?

Johanna come out and build a snowman?

Knock, knock.

Who's there?

Duncan.

Duncan who?

Duncan cookies in hot cocoa is delicious!

Q: Why wasn't a creature stirring on Christmas Eve?

A: Because they had already finished making their Christmas soup.

Joe: Did your goat eat my hat and mittens?

Jim: Yes, he scarfed them right down.

Q: What's as big as a polar bear but weighs nothing?

A: A polar bear's shadow

Q: Why wouldn't Rudolph leave the barn to guide the sleigh?

A: He was stalling.

- -

Q: What do porcupines say when they kiss under the mistletoe?

A: "Ouch!"

Q: What happened when the frog's snowmobile broke down?

A: It had to be toad away.

Q: What did Mrs. Claus say when Santa came home late?

A: "Where on earth have you been?"

Q: What did the fish think of its Christmas present?

A: She thought it was fin-tastic!

Q: What did Santa say when Mrs. Claus made him coffee?

A: "Thanks a latte!"

Q: What do you get when you cross a duck and a squirrel?

A: A nut-quacker

Q: What do you get when you cross a reindeer and a fish?

A: Ru-dolphin

Q: Why was the skunk put on Santa's naughty list?

A: Because he was a stinker.

Jack: Why did you give me worms for Christmas?

Jeff: Because they were dirt cheap!

Q: What do you do if a polar bear is in your bed?

A: Find a hotel for the night!

Q: What do you get if you cross a turtle and a snowman?

A: A snow-poke

Q: What did the Dalmatian say after Christmas dinner?

A: "That hit the spot!"

Q: How do you feel after drinking hot cocoa?

A: Marsh-mellow

Q: How do you know if there's a polar bear in your refrigerator?

A: The door won't close!

Q: How do alligators cook their Christmas dinner?

A: In a croc-pot

Q: What do you get when you cross a pine tree with a hyena?

A: An ever-grin tree

Q: What do you get if you put your head in the punch bowl?

A: Egg-noggin

Q: **What's the best thing to drink on Christmas Eve?**

A: Nativi-tea

Q: **What do you get when you cross a squirrel and a Christmas pirate?**

A: Treasure chestnuts roasting on an open fire

Q: **What do you get when an astronaut goes skiing?**

A: An ava-launch

Q: **What did one skier say to the other skier?**

A: "It's all downhill from here."

Q: **What's Santa's favorite book?**

A: *Merry Poppins*

Q: **What kind of dinosaur hibernates for the winter?**

A: A bronto-snore-us

Q: **Why did the child need new glasses for Christmas?**

A: He didn't have visions of sugarplums dancing in his head.

Q: **What do reindeer have that no other animals have?**

A: Baby reindeer

Q: **Did you hear about the cat who chewed on the Christmas lights?**

A: It was shocking!

Q: Did you hear about the Christmas star?

A: It's out of this world.

Q: Why couldn't the fish go Christmas shopping?

A: It didn't have anemone.

Q: How do you spell *frozen* with only three letters?

A: *I-C-E!*

Q: What kind of snowmobile does a farmer like to ride?

A: A Cow-asaki

Q: How does a grizzly get through the holidays?

A: He grins and bears it.

Q: **How did the wise men sneak across the desert?**

A: They had camel-flage.

Q: **What do you get when a polar bear sits on a pumpkin?**

A: Squash

Q: **How do you pay when you're Christmas shopping?**

A: With jingle bills

Q: **What kind of toy does a chicken want for Christmas?**

A: A Jack-in-the-bok-bok-box!

Q: How does an opera singer make Christmas cookies?

A: With icing (I sing)

Brother: I broke my candy cane in two places.

Sister: Then don't go to those places anymore!

Julie: Did you have fun at the Christmas party?

Josie: No, it was a Feliz Navi-dud.

Q: How do you invite a fish to your Christmas party?

A: Drop it a line.

Q: **What did Santa say when he parked his sleigh?**

A: "There's snow place like home."

Q: **Why did the snowman need dandruff shampoo?**

A: Because he had snowflakes.

Knock, knock.

Who's there?

Window.

Window who?

Window you want to open your Christmas presents?

Q: **Why did the girl give the boy an orange for Christmas?**

A: Because he was her main squeeze.

Q: What do you get when you hang a turkey from the fireplace?

A: A stocking stuffer

Q: Why did the girl get celery for Christmas?

A: It was a stalk-ing stuffer.

Knock, knock.

Who's there?

Don.

Don who?

Don you want to come out and play in the snow?

Knock, knock.

Who's there?

Sarah.

Sarah who?

Sarah reason you're not having any Christmas cookies?

Knock, knock.

Who's there?

Funnel.

Funnel who?

The funnel start once everyone shows up to the party!

Brother: Is this present from Mom?

Sister: Ap-parent-ly it is!

Q: What's a cow's favorite Christmas song?

A: "Jingle Bulls"

Q: What is an elf's favorite dessert?

A: Shortbread cookies

Knock, knock.

Who's there?

Braydon.

Braydon who?

Are you Braydon your hair for the

Christmas party?

Q: How does Santa get into his chalet?

A: With a s-key (ski)

Q: What do you put in a hyena's

Christmas stocking?

A: A Snickers bar

Q: Why was the snowman so mean?

A: Because he was coldhearted.

Q: What do you get when you mix Rudolph and the queen?

A: A reign-deer

Knock, knock.

Who's there?

Police.

Police who?

Police come over for Christmas dinner!

Knock, knock.

Who's there?

Ice cream.

Ice cream who?

Ice cream when I see the abominable snowman!

Q: **What do you get when you combine a snowball, a fish, and a Christmas tree branch?**

A: A frozen fish stick

Knock, knock.

Who's there?

Megan.

Megan who?

It's Megan me crazy having to wait to open my presents!

Knock, knock.

Who's there?

Glove.

Glove who?

I glove the holidays.

Q: Why does Santa like his sleigh?

A: Because it's satis-flying.

Q: Why do reindeer eat so many candy canes?

A: For nourish-mint

Q: Why did the snowman get a headache?

A: He had brain freeze.

Q: Why did Santa's reindeer go to jail?

A: For Comet-ting a crime

Q: What kind of dogs saw the Christmas star?

A: German shepherds

Q: Why couldn't the conductor drive the Polar Express?

A: He didn't have enough training.

Q: How do pirates save money on their Christmas shopping?

A: They look for sails.

Q: Why did Santa go back for more dessert?

A: Because he wanted to retreat.

Q: How does a sailor get to church on Christmas Eve?

A: On his wor-ship

Tongue Twisters

Round red wreath.

Striped stuffed stockings.

Green glitter glue.

Santa sings silly sleigh songs.

Q: Why did the dog always get depressed at Christmas?

A: Because the holidays were ruff.

Cassie: Did the cow like the present you got him?

Kendra: No, he thought it was udderly ridiculous.

Knock, knock.

Who's there?

Ville.

Ville who?

No, the opposite: it's Whoville.

Knock, knock.

Who's there?

Hammond.

Hammond who?

Hammond eggs taste great on

Christmas morning.

Q: Why was the farmer on Santa's naughty list?

A: Because his pig squealed on him!

Q: What do you call a twig that doesn't like Christmas?

A: A stick-in-the-mud

Q: How did the turkey get home for Christmas?

A: In a gravy boat

Q: Why do baseball players love Christmas dinner?

A: They like to be behind the plate.

Q: What is a squirrel's favorite part of the Christmas season?

A: Going to see *The Nutcracker*

Billy: I got my pig some soap for Christmas.

Ben: That's hogwash!

Knock, knock.

Who's there?

Lion.

Lion who?

I'd be lion if I told you I didn't love the holidays.

Q: How do you make a strawberry shake?

A: Introduce it to the abominable snowman.

Knock, knock.

Who's there?

Weed.

Weed who?

Weed better leave for the Christmas party or we'll be late!

Knock, knock.

Who's there?

Kenya.

Kenya who?

Kenya tell me your favorite Christmas tradition?

Q: Why did the moon get sick after eating Christmas dinner?

A: Because it was so full.

Q: **Which baseball player makes the best Christmas cakes?**

A: The batter

Q: **How do the Christmas angels greet each other?**

A: They say, "Halo."

Q: **What happened when the rabbit ate too many Christmas cookies?**

A: It was hopped up on sugar.

Q: **Why don't crabs spend much money for Christmas?**

A: Because they're penny-pinchers.

Q: Why don't hyenas get sick in the winter?

A: Because laughter is the best medicine.

Sally: What if Jimmy can't play the trumpet in the Christmas concert?

Suzie: We'll find a substi-toot.

Q: Why did the boy hang triangles on his Christmas tree?

A: So he could have a geome-tree.

Q: What do reindeer like to eat with their spaghetti?

A: Meat-bells

Luke: Does Santa like to study chemistry?

Stew: Only periodically.

Knock, knock.

Who's there?

Dozen.

Dozen who?

Dozen anyone want to sing a Christmas carol?

Knock, knock.

Who's there?

Reindeer.

Reindeer who?

It's going to reindeer, so you'd better bring an umbrella.

Q: Why do hummingbirds hum Christmas carols?

A: Because they can't remember the words.

Q: How do ducks celebrate New Year's Eve?

A: With fire-quackers

Q: What is something that's easy to catch in the winter, but hard to throw?

A: A cold

Q: Why did the raisin stay home from the Christmas party?

A: Because it couldn't find a date.

Knock, knock.

Who's there?

Orange.

Orange who?

Orange you glad Christmas is almost here?

Q: What kind of fruit decorates a

Christmas tree?

A: A pineapple

Q: Why did the orange stop

Christmas shopping?

A: Because it ran out of juice.

Q: What do you get when your dog plays too

long in the snow?

A: A pup-sicle

Knock, knock.

Who's there?

Candice.

Candice who?

Candice holiday season get any better?

Knock, knock.

Who's there?

Juan.

Juan who?

Juan a kiss under the mistletoe?

Knock, knock.

Who's there?

Minnow.

Minnow who?

Let minnow if you can't make it to the Christmas party.

Q: What happened when the cucumber ran out of wrapping paper?

A: It left him in a pickle.

Susie: Is your Christmas gift here yet?

Sally: Yes, it's present.

Caleb: Do you like the red frosting on my Christmas cookies?

Callie: Yes, it's to dye for.

Q: What does Santa use for a map?

A: A snow globe

Q: Why do kids get bad grades during the holidays?

A: Because it's D-cember.

Q: What did Santa say when the elf told a funny joke?

A: "You sleigh me!"

Q: What do you give a rabbit for Christmas?

A: A hare-brush

- -

Q: What do you give a flea for Christmas?

A: An Itch A Sketch

Q: Why did the boy get a bucket for Christmas?

A: Because he looked a little pail.

Stanley: Did your dad like the statue you gave him for Christmas?

Henry: No, it was a bust.

Eva: Did you know Santa's suit is exactly the right size?

Ava: Well, that's fitting.

Q: Why do snowmen wear sunglasses?

A: To keep the sun out of their ice.

Anna: Should we get Dad a drill for Christmas?

Ella: No, that's boring.

Q: Why is Christmas so exciting?

A: Because it's an advent-ure.

Q: Why won't Santa wear an itchy scarf?

A: Because it's a pain in the neck.

Q: How did Santa feel about the house with the security system?

A: He was alarmed!

Q: Where did Noah like to go in the winter?

A: All the way to the ark-tic

Q: How does Santa know what to give a zebra for Christmas?

A: The answer is black and white.

Josie: You forgot the lamb for the nativity scene!

Jamie: Well, I feel sheepish.

Q: Why can't Martians get along at Christmas?

A: Because they're alienated from one another.

Q: When is it hard to hear a Christmas movie?

A: When it's ani-muted

Q: How did Santa feel when he got soot on his suit?

A: He felt ash-amed.

Lucy: Are you allowed to make up a Christmas story?

Lena: Yes, I'm authorized.

Q: What does a ghost think about Christmas carols?

A: It thinks they're boo-tiful.

Q: How does a wolf like its Christmas cookies?

A: Bite-sized.

Tory: Why did Santa put tuna in my stocking?

Terry: He thought it would be bene-fish-ial.

Q: Why do elves like to go camping?

A: Because they're so compe-tent.

Q: Why don't we go camping in the winter?

A: Because it's too in-tents.

**Q: How do you know when a snowman doesn't
like you?**

A: He'll give you the cold shoulder.

**Jane: My mom won't let me embroider my
Christmas stocking!**

Jill: Well, that's crewel!

Q: Why did Mrs. Claus give Rudolph a hug?

A: Because he was so deer.

Q: Why was the beaver so sad at Christmas?

A: Because his present was dam-aged.

Q: Why did the elf have to clean up after the reindeer?

A: Because it was his doody.

Q: Why do cows like to sing Christmas carols?

A: Because they're so moo-sical.

Q: Why do elves always wear perfume?

A: They think it's e-scent-ial.

Q: What did Luke Skywalker say at Christmas dinner?

A: "May the fork be with you."

Q: Why did Santa fly his sleigh through the Grand Canyon?

A: He thought it was gorge-ous.

Q: When does sledding make you laugh?

A: When it's hill-arious

Q: How do cows pay for their Christmas shopping?

A: With their moo-lah

Q: When can't you put any jelly in your stocking?

A: When it's already jam-packed.

Q: Why shouldn't the reindeer make fun of Rudolph's nose?

A: Because it's impo-light.

Darla: When should we sing Christmas carols?

Debby: Hymn-ediately!

Q: Why is Santa so jolly?

A: Because he's a good fellow.

Q: Which size cup of hot cocoa tastes the best?

A: A medi-yum

Mrs. Claus: I ironed your Santa suit for Christmas Eve.

Santa: I'm impressed!

Q: Why was the chef late for Christmas dinner?

A: He ran out of thyme.

Q: What do you call a great snowplow driver?

A: Wreckless

Q: What happens if you see a polar bear at the shopping center?

A: You might get mall-ed.

Q: How do you see an ice-cream cone from far away?

A: Use a tele-scoop.

Q: What does a hen have for dessert at Christmas?

A: Layer cake

Q: How did the wise men know to follow the star?

A: They had frankin-sense.

Q: How do you make your Christmas cards unique?

A: You put your own stamp on them.

Q: Why were the reindeer mad at Santa?

A: He drove them up the wall.

Q: Why did two skunks give each other the same present?

A: Because great minds stink alike.

Q: Does Santa worry about delivering all the presents?

A: No, he's got it in the bag.

Q: How did the Three Little Pigs stay merry at Christmas?

A: They kept their chinny-chin-chins up.

Q: **When does Santa deliver presents to the sheep?**

A: Last but not fleeced

Kelly: Will Santa bring my dog a present?

Karly: Make no bones about it.

Q: **What did Santa say to the naughty squirrel?**

A: "If you can't say something nice, don't say nuttin' at all."

Q: **How did the canary afford all her Christmas gifts?**

A: She used her nest egg.

Curtis: Are you excited to put up the Christmas tree?

Carter: Yes, I'm on pines and needles!

Gary: Is this star too fancy for our Christmas tree?

Mary: Yes, I think it's over-the-top.

Q: Why doesn't Blitzen ever get in trouble?

A: He's always passing the buck.

Q: Why is everyone happy at the North Pole?

A: Because they're on top of the world.

Q: Why does Santa keep a hammer in his sleigh on Christmas Eve?

A: So he can beat the clock.

Q: When will Santa come down the chimney?

A: In the Nick of time

Q: When should you open your Christmas gifts?

A: There's no time like the present.

Q: Why won't you ever see the gingerbread man cry?

A: Because he's one tough cookie.

Bobby: Santa makes you mad?

Billy: Yes, every time he's here I see red.

Q: Why did the mittens get married?

A: It was glove at first sight.

Q: When do you bring lipstick under the mistletoe?

A: If you want to kiss and makeup.

Q: Why did the elf bring his garbage on a date to the movies?

A: He wanted to take out the trash.

Q: Where do you keep your Santa suit?

A: In the Santa Claus-et

Q: When does a weatherman need an umbrella?

A: When his Christmas cookies have sprinkles

Q: Why did Santa hire an elephant for his workshop?

A: Because it would work for peanuts.

Q: How does a chicken get to the Christmas party?

A: In a heli-coop-ter

Q: Why did the pig look great at the Christmas party?

A: Because it was so sty-lish.

Q: How is a wool cardigan like a guy at the gym?

A: They're both heavy sweaters.

Q: Are the reindeer excited about the Christmas party?

A: Yes, they'll be there with bells on.

Grandma: Did Jimmy like the soccer ball I gave him for Christmas?

Grandpa: He got a kick out of it.

Q: What do sharks eat for Christmas dessert?

A: Octo-pie

Ralphie: Why did you give me lettuce for Christmas?

Alfie: You said you wanted to get ahead.

Q: How did Dorothy know what to give the Scarecrow for Christmas?

A: It was a no-brainer.

Q: Why did the boy keep asking for a train for Christmas?

A: He had a one-track mind.

Q: **What did the alien think about his Christmas present?**

A: He thought it was out of this world.

Q: **What do polar bears want for breakfast on Christmas morning?**

A: Grrrr-nola

Q: **What do you get when you cross a reindeer and a ghost?**

A: A cari-boo

Knock, knock.

Who's there?

Alpine.

Alpine who?

Alpine trees look great with Christmas lights.

Q: What did the pirate say when he was freezing in the snow?

A: "Shiver me timbers!"

Q: What game do you give a mouse for Christmas?

A: Par-cheesy

Q: Why can't ponies sing Christmas carols?

A: Because they're a little horse.

Toby: I ruined the treats for Christmas.

Tommy: Oh, fudge!

Q: When is a puppy like a cold winter's day?

A: When it's nippy

Q: Why did the Easter Bunny go trick-or-treating at Christmas?

A: He was in a holi-daze.

Q: Why would you give away a fireplace for free?

A: You must have a big hearth.

Q: What happens if you give a snowman a carrot?

A: He'll get nosy.

Q: Why won't penguins use cell phones?

A: Because they're cold-fashioned.

Q: What do you call Santa when his suit is wrinkled?

A: Kris Krinkle

Sara: Why won't your parents eat almonds at Christmastime?

Dora: They're nuts.

Q: What will happen if you run out of peppermints?

A: People will raise cane!

Q: Why was Santa sad?

A: He didn't think his parents believed in him.

Q: Why couldn't Rudolph buy any more soap?

A: He was all washed-up.

Q: What did the snowplow driver say at the end of the season?

A: "It was nice snowing you."

Q: What's a turkey's favorite Christmas dessert?

A: Bluberry gobbler

Q: Why couldn't the elf pay for her Christmas shopping?

A: She was a little short.

Q: **What happened when the reindeer flew into a mountain?**

A: They couldn't get over it.

Knock, knock.

Who's there?

Alpaca.

Alpaca who?

Alpaca bag and visit Grandma for Christmas.

Q: **Why shouldn't you do homework while you're ice-skating?**

A: Your grades might slip.

Jeremy: Why do you believe in Santa Claus?

Jillian: Because the Easter Bunny and the tooth fairy told me he's real.

Q: What did the rabbit say to the frog?

A: "Hoppy Holidays!"

Wyatt: Did you hear we're just having sandwiches for Christmas dinner?

William: That's a bunch of baloney!

Q: What does a frog say when it's unwrapping its Christmas presents?

A: "Rip it, rip it, rip it."

Q: Why wouldn't the skeleton go snowboarding down the mountain?

A: He didn't have the guts.

Olivia: Did you know lots of reindeer live in Alaska?

Violet: That's what I herd.

Aunt Sue: Is Alex disappointed that he caught a cold at Christmas?

Uncle Sam: He'll get over it.

Bess: Do you like the trampoline Santa gave you for Christmas?

Tess: I'm jumping for joy!

Q: Why was the dog barking at the fireplace?

A: It made him hot under the collar.

Tracy: Was your mom surprised when she got a rug for Christmas?

Trudy: She was floored!

Q: Why did Santa give Humpty Dumpty a lot of presents?

A: Because he's a good egg.

Q: Why did the snowman take a carrot to the library?

A: So he could put his nose in a book.

Q: How is Santa's beard like a Christmas tree?

A: They both need trimming.

Q: When does King Arthur do his Christmas shopping?

A: At knight

Q: How do dogs play Christmas carols?

A: On a trombone

Q: Why was the cookie so excited to see its family at Christmas?

A: Because it was a wafer such a long time.

Q: Why did the hotdog keep telling jokes at the Christmas talent show?

A: Because it was on a roll.

Q: Why did the snowman go to the dentist?

A: He wanted his teeth whitened.

Q: What happens when a polar bear is all alone?

A: He's feels ice-olated.

Peter: Do you think we should read a Christmas story?

Tyler: That's a novel idea!

Q: What happened when the elf showed up to work in flip-flops?

A: Santa gave him the boot!

Knock, knock.

Who's there?

Europe.

Europe who?

Europe late waiting for Santa Claus!

Q: What kind of bird is sad when Christmas is over?

A: A bluebird

Q: Why was the elf yelling?

A: Because he stubbed his mistletoe.

Knock, knock.

Who's there?

Cook.

Cook who?

Clearly the holidays are making you a little crazy!

Knock, knock.

Who's there?

Avery.

Avery who?

Avery nice person wished me Merry Christmas today.

Q: What game do elves like to play when they're not making toys?

A: Gift tag

Knock, knock.

Who's there?

Abby.

Abby who?

Abby New Year!

Q: How do snowmen make friends at parties?

A: They know how to break the ice.

Q: How do you get a polar bear's attention?

A: With a cold snap

Knock, knock.

Who's there?

Figs.

Figs who?

Can you figs the star on the Christmas tree?

Q: Why do you sing lullabies to a snowbank?

A: So it can drift off to sleep.

Tony: I don't think we'll finish our Christmas story on time.

Tammy: We'll have to book it!

Knock, knock.

Who's there?

Jewel.

Jewel who?

Jewel feel sick if you eat too many candy canes.

Knock, knock.

Who's there?

Left hand.

Left hand who?

I left hand forgot my scarf and mittens.

Knock, knock.

Who's there?

Wendy.

Wendy who?

Wendy snow falls, we can go sledding.

Knock, knock.

Who's there?

Sticker.

Sticker who?

Sticker presents under the tree before

Christmas Eve!

Knock, knock.

Who's there?

Rooster.

Rooster who?

Rooster turkey in the oven for

Christmas dinner.

Knock, knock.

Who's there?

Firewood.

Firewood who?

A firewood warm things up in here.

LAUGH
-Out-
LOUD

ADVENTURE

JOKES
for KIDS

To the international students who have shared their lives with me these past few years: Rita, David M, Icey, Jonita, Hayeong, Stefanie, Lucero, Kairu, David, and Michael. Knowing you is the best kind of adventure!

Q: Why were there lizards all over the bathroom wall?

A: Because it had been rep-tiled.

Q: How do you call an alligator?

A: You croco-dial your phone.

Knock, knock.

Who's there?

Wildebeest.

Wildebeest who?

Wildebeest marry Belle at the end of the story?

Knock, knock.

Who's there?

Parmesan.

Parmesan who?

Do I have your parmesan to come in?

Q: What do you call a squid with only six arms?

A: A hexa-pus.

Q: How does the runner like her eggs?

A: With a dash of pepper.

Knock, knock.

Who's there?

Wanda.

Wanda who?

Wanda go hiking with me?

Q: Why did the clock go to jail?

A: For killing time!

Q: Why did the butcher work so hard?

A: He had to bring home the bacon.

Q: Why did the polar bear spit out the clown?

A: He tasted funny.

Knock, knock.

Who's there?

Joanna.

Joanna who?

Joanna go to the races today?

Q: Why did the sea captain throw

peanut butter in the ocean?

A: He wanted to attract the jellyfish.

Q: What do you get when you cross an

astronaut and a sea creature?

A: A starfish.

Q: What's a sailor's least favorite vegetable?

A: A leek.

Knock, knock.

Who's there?

Llama.

Llama who?

Llama in! It's cold out here!

Knock, knock.

Who's there?

Wooden shoe.

Wooden shoe who?

Wooden shoe like to go canoeing today?

Q: What kind of vegetables wear socks?

A: Potatoes.

Q: Why don't fish ever go on vacation?

A: Because they're always in schools.

Q: What kind of snake leads the band?

A: A boa conductor.

Q: What is a grasshopper's favorite sport?

A: Cricket.

Q: Why do babies like basketball?

A: They're always dribbling.

Parent: How was school today?

Child: There was a kidnapping in our class today.

Parent: Oh, no! What happened?

Child: The teacher woke him up and gave him detention.

Q: What kind of grades did the ship captain get?

A: High Cs.

Q: How do you throw a party on Mars?

A: You planet.

Knock, knock.

Who's there?

Wool.

Wool who?

Wool you go on an adventure with me?

Knock, knock.

Who's there?

Philip.

Philip who?

Philip the car and we can be on our way.

Q: What do boxers do when they're thirsty?

A: They get some punch.

Knock, knock.

Who's there?

Joe King.

Joe King who?

Oh, no one. I'm just joking.

Q: What did the man do when he was standing out in a thunderstorm?

A: He hailed a cab.

Q: **What is an ape's favorite kind of cookie?**

A: Chocolate chimp.

Q: **Where do you park your rocket on Mars?**

A: At a parking meteor.

Q: **What did the horse do after the trail ride?**

A: It hit the hay.

Q: **Why did the kids always fight during math class?**

A: There was division among them.

Q: What do bakers and cats have in common?

A: They both like to start from scratch.

Q: What do you get if you put a pig on a racetrack?

A: A road hog!

Q: What did the computer programmer do at lunchtime?

A: She had a byte.

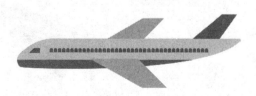

Q: Why are night crawlers so smart?

A: They're bookworms.

Q: Why did the clock get in trouble?

A: It wouldn't stop tocking.

Q: Where do tarantulas get their information?

A: From the World Wide Web.

Q: Why did the toilet go to the doctor?

A: It looked flushed!

Q: Why did the karate instructor wear earplugs?

A: He had sensei-tive ears.

Q: What did the leopard say after dinner?

A: That hit the spot.

Q: How do you get a baby astronaut to stop crying?

A: You rocket!

Q: How does an elephant get ready for vacation?

A: It packs its trunk.

Q: **Why did the maple tree watch romantic movies?**

A: It was sappy.

Q: **Who is the best dancer at the monsters' ball?**

A: The boogieman.

Q: **Why did the snickerdoodle refuse to be eaten?**

A: It was one tough cookie.

Q: **Why did the pony get in trouble?**

A: It was horsing around.

Knock, knock.

Who's there?

Iguana.

Iguana who?

Iguana go mountain climbing with you!

Q: What is a black belt's favorite drink?

A: Kara-tea.

Knock, knock.

Who's there?

Russian.

Russian who?

I'm Russian around to get ready!

Q: What did the atom do when it was ready to go?

A: It split.

Q: What kind of shoes do ninjas wear?

A: Sneakers.

Q: Why did the man quit being a dentist?

A: He didn't have the patients for it.

Q: Why did the chicken travel the world?

A: It was tired of being cooped up!

Q: When do ducks get out of bed?

A: At the quack of dawn.

Q: Why couldn't the librarian ever go on vacation?

A: She was always booked.

Q: How did the monkey escape from the zoo?

A: In a hot-air baboon.

Q: **Why did the robot go on a camping trip?**

A: To recharge its batteries.

Q: **Why was it so windy in the football stadium?**

A: There were thousands of fans!

Q: **Why did the pelican run out of money?**

A: It had a big bill.

Q: **Why was the valley laughing?**

A: Because the mountains were hill-arious!

Knock, knock.

Who's there?

Funnel.

Funnel who?

The funnel start once we head to the beach.

Q: Why did the student do his home-work in a helicopter?

A: He wanted a higher education.

Q: How do you make a strawberry shake?

A: Tell it a scary story.

Q: What did the horse say to the cowboy when it ran out of hay?

A: That's the last straw!

Q: What do you get when a butcher and a baker get married?

A: Meat loaf.

Knock, knock.

Who's there?

Radio.

Radio who?

Radio not, here we come!

Q: What is the easiest kind of lid to open?

A: Your eyelid.

Q: How do mountains stay warm in the winter?

A: With their snowcaps.

Q: Why did the boy bring his computer to the beach?

A: He wanted to surf the internet.

Q: How did the polar bear get to work?

A: On a motor-icicle.

Q: Why did the duck go skydiving?

A: It wasn't chicken!

Knock, knock.

Who's there?

Europe.

Europe who?

Europe very early this morning.

Q: When are all the books in the library the same color?

A: When they're read.

Q: What do you get when you cross a bicycle and a flower?

A: A bike petal.

Q: What did the sailor say every morning?

A: "Seas the day!"

Q: What is a whale's favorite vegetable?

A: A sea cucumber.

Q: What do you get when your dad rides a bike?

A: A pop-cycle.

Q: Why do surgeons make great comedians?

A: Because they always have you in stitches.

Q: What do you call a dancing sheep?

A: A baaa-llerina.

Q: Where did the skiers fall in love?

A: At the snowball.

Q: Why did the cow become an acro-bat?

A: It was so flexi-bull!

Q: How does Santa find his way home?

A: He uses his snow globe.

Q: How do you catch a school of fish?

A: With a bookworm.

Q: What do grizzlies do when they meet a clown?

A: They just grin and bear it!

Andy: Did you hear about the panther that told the boy he wouldn't eat him?

Daniel: No, what happened?

Andy: He was lion.

Q: Where do tropical fish keep their work?

A: In a reef-case.

Q: What happened when Frankenstein heard the joke?

A: He was in stitches!

Q: What do bananas and acrobats have in common?

A: They can both do splits.

Q: Where can you learn how to make a banana split?

A: Sundae school.

Q: What do you call it when two boa constrictors fall in love?

A: A crush.

Knock, knock.

Who's there?

Wood.

Wood who?

Wood you like to go swimming with me?

Q: Why did the dog get kicked out of the soccer game?

A: He was playing too ruff!

Knock, knock.

Who's there?

Justin.

Justin who?

Justin time to go snowboarding!

Knock, knock.

Who's there?

Noah.

Noah who?

Noah great place to go camping?

Q: Why did the hungry lion eat the dentist?

A: He looked so filling.

Knock, knock.

Who's there?

Howard.

Howard who?

Howard you like to go on a safari?

Q: Why can't you give your dog the TV remote?

A: It'll keep hitting the paws button.

Q: Why did the snail take a nap?

A: It was feeling sluggish.

Q: What do you call a sleepy wood-cutter?

A: A slumber-jack.

Q: Why was the climbing rope anxious?

A: It was getting all strung out!

Q: How did Mary feel when her little lamb followed her to school?

A: Sheepish!

Q: Why was the scuba diver embarrassed?

A: He saw the ocean's bottom.

Q: Why wouldn't the chicken grow?

A: It had smallpox.

Knock, knock.

Who's there?

Peter.

Peter who?

Peter boots on so we can go hiking!

Q: **What do you give a farmer who sings out of tune?**

A: A pitchfork.

Knock, knock.

Who's there?

Muffin.

Muffin who?

Muffin to do today—let's go have some fun!

Q: **What's a robot's favorite snack?**

A: Computer chips.

Q: Why do snowmen melt if you take their carrots away?

A: It makes them boiling mad!

Knock, knock.

Who's there?

Luke.

Luke who?

Luke over there—a bear is coming!

Q: What do you get when a T. rex and a brontosaurus play football?

A: Dino-scores.

Luke: I'm so tired of climbing this big hill!

Zack: Oh, get over it!

Q: Why did the whales watch the sunset?

A: They wanted a sea-nic view.

Q: Why did the baker become an actor?

A: He wanted to play a roll.

Q: Why did the vampire join the circus?

A: He wanted to be an acro-bat.

Q: What is the biggest bug in the world?

A: The mam-moth.

Q: Why did the coffee file a police report?

A: It was mugged.

Knock, knock.

Who's there?

Dishes.

Dishes who?

Dishes the police. Come out with your hands up!

Q: What do you get when you cross a knife and your front lawn?

A: Blades of grass!

Knock, knock.

Who's there?

Norway.

Norway who?

Norway am I parachute jumping out of a plane!

Q: How does a polar bear build its house?

A: Igloos it together.

Q: Where does Mickey Mouse keep his groceries?

A: In a Minnie fridge.

Q: What happened when the turkey and the rooster got in a fight?

A: The turkey got the stuffing knocked out of him.

Tom: Hey, want to hear another insect joke?

Jim: No, stop bugging me!

Q: Why did the lumberjack get fired?

A: He axed too many questions.

Q: What do conductors and mountain climbers have in common?

A: They both like the terrain.

Q: What do ghosts wear to climb a mountain?

A: Hiking boo-ts!

Q: What do you get when you cross a dog and a cow?

A: Hound beef.

Q: What is the most famous kind of drink?

A: A celebri-tea!

Q: How did the fisherman finish in half the time?

A: He was e-fish-ent!

Q: Why do skeletons always laugh at your jokes?

A: They find everything humerus.

Q: How do you light things in a stadium?

A: With a soccer match.

Q: How do snowmen stay warm at night?

A: With a blanket of snow.

Q: How did the fisherman have his tonsils taken out?

A: He went to a sturgeon.

Q: What do you get if you put coffee on your head?

A: A cap-puccino.

Q: Why did the man put his car in the oven?

A: He wanted to drive a hot rod.

Q: How did the pepper catch a cold?

A: It was a little chili.

Q: How did the boulder go to bed?

A: He rocked himself to sleep.

Q: What do you get if you cross a pillow and a can of soda?

A: A soft drink!

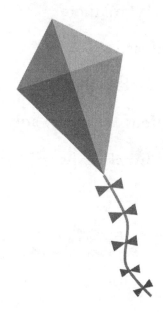

Q: What is the difference between a dog and a flea?

A: A dog can flea but a flea can't dog.

Q: Why was the dog laughing?

A: Someone gave it a funny bone.

Knock, knock.

Who's there?

Defeat.

Defeat who?

Defeat are really sore after a long hike!

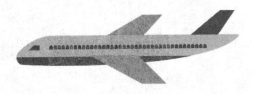

Knock, knock.

Who's there?

Anita.

Anita who?

Anita get out of the house for some fresh air!

Q: What do baseball teams and bakers have in common?

A: They both need good batters.

Q: What's something you serve but can never eat?

A: A tennis ball.

Q: What did the shark do when it caught a cold?

A: It took some vitamin sea.

Knock, knock.

Who's there?

Wendy.

Wendy who?

Wendy we go to the skate park?

Knock, knock.

Who's there?

Pecan.

Pecan who?

Pecan someone your own size!

Q: What happened when the sea lions fell in love?

A: They sealed it with a kiss.

Q: What do bats do in their free time?

A: They just hang out!

Q: Why did the librarian become a detective?

A: She wanted to go undercover.

Q: Why shouldn't you tell jokes to an egg?

A: You don't want it to crack up!

Q: What happened when the dalmatian took a bath?

A: It became spotless.

Q: Why do frogs love baseball?

A: They like to catch the fly balls.

Q: Why did the baby become a scientist?

A: She liked her formulas.

Q: Where do swimmers go for fun?

A: To the dive-in movies.

Q: What do you call it when quarters rain from the sky?

A: Climate change!

Q: What's a grasshopper's favorite sport?

A: Cricket.

Knock, knock.

Who's there?

Alpaca.

Alpaca who?

Alpaca lunch for our hike today.

Q: What do you get when you cross a chicken and a dog?

A: A clucker spaniel.

Q: Why do boxers make bad comedians?

A: They always start with the punch line.

Q: Why did the man's jacket catch on fire?

A: It was a blazer.

Knock, knock.

Who's there?

Hugo.

Hugo who?

Hugo first and I'll follow!

Q: Why did the cowboy take his horse to the vet?

A: It had hay fever.

Q: What kind of shoes do butchers wear?

A: Meat loafers.

Q: What do race car drivers eat before they race?

A: Car-bohydrates.

Q: What gets harder to catch the faster you run?

A: Your breath.

Q: Why can't you win a race against a barber?

A: He knows all the shortcuts.

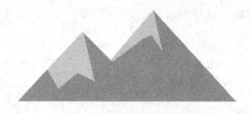

Q: What happened when the skunk wrote a book?

A: It became a best smeller!

Q: What do you get when you cross a turtle and a porcupine?

A: A slowpoke!

Knock, knock.

Who's there?

Donut.

Donut who?

Donut you want to come outside today?

Q: What happened to the boy who swallowed his trombone?

A: He tooted his own horn!

Q: What kind of fish likes bubble gum?

A: A blowfish.

Q: Why wouldn't the sheep stop talking?

A: It liked to ram-ble!

Q: Why did the spider steal the sports car?

A: He wanted to take it for a spin.

Q: Why did the sun move away from the moon?

A: It wanted some space.

Q: How come it didn't cost anything to go bungee jumping?

A: It was a free fall!

Q: What kind of clothes do dogs wear in the summer?

A: Pants.

Q: Where do scarecrows go for fun?

A: On field trips.

Q: Why are mountains always tired?

A: Because they don't Everest!

Knock, knock.

Who's there?

Sara.

Sara who?

Sara nother way around this lake?

Q: Why is tennis such a noisy sport?

A: The players raise a lot of racket.

Q: Why can't you play hide-and-seek

with mountains?

A: They're always peak-ing.

Knock, knock.

Who's there?

Taco.

Taco who?

Taco 'bout what you want to do today.

Q: What do you get when you cross an alien and a tea party?

A: Flying saucers.

Q: What do you get when you cross a pig and a toolbox?

A: A ham-mer.

Q: What do you call a banana store?

A: A monkey business!

Q: What do you get when you put an opera singer in the bathtub?

A: A soap-rano!

Q: Why did the chemistry teacher stop telling jokes?

A: He could never get a reaction.

Q: What are a horse's favorite snacks?

A: Straw-berries and hay-zelnuts.

Q: What do you call a boomerang that doesn't come back?

A: A stick.

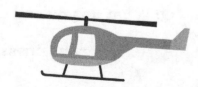

Q: How does a bug get around in the winter?

A: In a snowmo-beetle.

Q: How does a skater cut up her steak?

A: With Roller-blades!

Q: How do athletes stay cool in the summer?

A: They stay close to their fans.

Q: Why did the guitar player go to the auto mechanic?

A: She needed a tune-up.

Rita: Do you know where they cooked the first French fries?

Stephanie: France?

Rita: No, in Greece!

Q: Why did they kick the pig off the basketball court?

A: It was hogging the ball!

Sam: Why did the alien grow a garden in space?

Marcus: It had a green thumb!

Knock, knock.

Who's there?

Riley.

Riley who?

I Riley think you should wear a helmet if you skateboard!

Q: Why was the whale always painting?

A: It was art-sea.

Q: What does an astronaut do with a bar of soap?

A: She takes a meteor shower!

Q: How does a lobster like its eggs?

A: With a pinch of salt.

Knock, knock.

Who's there?

Toad.

Toad who?

I toad my mom we'd be back in time for dinner.

Knock, knock.

Who's there?

Avenue.

Avenue who?

Avenue seen the Grand Canyon before?

Susie: Want to go see the llamas?

Sofia: That sounds fun!

Susie: Alpaca suitcase.

Knock, knock.

Who's there?

Parker.

Parker who?

I parker bike in my garage.

Knock, knock.

Who's there?

Iguana.

Iguana who?

Iguana ride my scooter to the park today.

Knock, knock.

Who's there?

Harry.

Harry who?

Harry up so we can get going!

Knock, knock.

Who's there?

Finley.

Finley who?

Finley it's Saturday—let's go have some fun!

Knock, knock.

Who's there?

Toby.

Toby who?

Toby safe, wear a life jacket when you're sailing.

Knock, knock.

Who's there?

Heidi.

Heidi who?

Heidi picnic basket so the bears don't get it!

Knock, knock.

Who's there?

Sawyer.

Sawyer who?

I sawyer sister at the park today!

Jim: I want to canoe down the river today.

Sue: You otter do that!

Q: Why did the whale need a hug?

A: It was blue.

Q: Why did the driver squeeze his car?

A: Because it was a lemon.

Q: What do sharks eat for breakfast?

A: Muf-fins.

Q: Why did the baker make so much bread?

A: Because it was kneaded.

Q: What do you get when you put glue on your doughnut?

A: A paste-ry.

Q: How many skunks does it take to change a lightbulb?

A: Just a phew.

Q: What makes a pirate angry?

A: When you take away the P.

Hannah: There's an octopus in my bathtub!

Olivia: You're just squid-ing me.

Q: Why didn't the hunter eat sandwiches anymore?

A: He quit cold turkey.

Q: How did the scientist freshen up his lab?

A: He used experi-mints.

Q: What's an astronaut's favorite kind of cookie?

A: Rocket chip.

Knock, knock.

Who's there?

Irish.

Irish who?

Irish we would go on more adventures!

Tim: Hey, Mark. You want to hear my underwear joke?

Mark: Is it clean?

Q: **What word has three letters and starts with gas?**

A: A car.

Q: **Why did the girl join the soccer team?**

A: She thought she'd get a kick out of it.

Q: **What's a guitar player's favorite sport?**

A: Bass-jumping

Q: **Where do you put fish once you catch them?**

A: In a cof-fin.

Q: Why did the student run around the school before a test?

A: To jog her memory.

Q: Why don't crocodiles ever get lost?

A: They're great navi-gators.

Q: Why are story writers always cold?

A: They always have drafts on their desks.

Q: What kind of vegetable do hippos like?

A: Zoo-cchini.

Q: What kind of fruits do boxers eat?

A: Black-and-blue berries.

Q: What do you call a ram that tells a lot of jokes?

A: A silly goat.

Q: **How did the conductor get to work?**

A: On the bandwagon.

Q: **What did the sharks say at the all-you-can-eat buffet?**

A: Let's dive in!

Q: **What do you get when you cross a pilot and a swimming pool?**

A: A skydiver!

Q: **Why did the fisher run out of money?**

A: He couldn't keep his business afloat.

Knock, knock.

Who's there?

Rugby.

Rugby who?

My rugby needing some vacuuming today!

Q: Why wouldn't the bike wake up?

A: It was two tired.

Q: What do you get when you cross a pig and a tree?

A: A porcupine.

Q: What kind of bug is hard to catch?

A: A Fris-bee.

222

Q: How did the koala build its house?

A: With its bear hands.

Knock, knock.

Who's there?

Canopy.

Canopy who?

Canopy outside when we go camping?

Q: What do a judge and a tennis player have in common?

A: They both go to court every day.

Q: How many golfers does it take to change a lightbulb?

A: Fore!

Q: **What do you get when you cross an ox and a canoe?**

A: A ka-yak.

Q: **What do you call it when two black belts fall in love?**

A: Martial hearts.

Q: **Why did the secret agent get fired?**

A: He was clue-less.

Q: **What happened when the tigers escaped from the zoo?**

A: It became a cat-astrophe!

Q: What is a skunk's favorite color?

A: Pew-ter.

Q: Why did the detective fall asleep at his desk?

A: He had a pillow-case.

Q: What do eagles eat for lunch?

A: Fish and chirps.

Q: Where do you keep your pillow when you're camping?

A: In a knapsack.

What do you call a mountain climber?

Cliff.

What do you call a fisherman?

Rod.

What do you call a barber?

Harry.

What do you call a housekeeper?

Dustin.

What do you call a cat burglar?

Rob.

What do you call a librarian?

Paige.

What do you call a basketball player?

Duncan.

What do you call a weight lifter?

Jim.

What do you call a painter?

Art.

What do you call an archaeologist?

Doug.

Q: Why did the cowboy go crazy?

A: He was de-ranged.

Knock, knock.

Who's there?

Firewood.

Firewood who?

Firewood keep us warm when we're camping.

Q: What do you get if you put bananas in your tent?

A: Slipping bags!

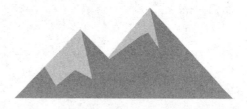

Q: Why did the girl take a blender on a hike?

A: So she could make trail mix.

Q: What kind of bird builds skyscrapers?

A: The crane.

Knock, knock.

Who's there?

Mustache.

Mustache who?

I mustache you if we can go rock climbing today!

Q: How much did it cost to build the beaver dam?

A: An arm and a log.

Q: Why didn't the fisherman get his email?

A: He was out of net-work.

Q: Why do baseball umpires always get dessert?

A: They're good at cleaning their plates.

Q: What do you get when you cross a washing machine and a bike?

A: A spin cycle!

Q: Why did the dentist coach the basketball team?

A: He knew the drills.

Q: To what type of fish should you never tell a secret?

A: A largemouth bass!

Q: What do you do with a worn-out baseball?

A: You pitch it.

Q: Why do farmers like to jump rope?

A: They never skip a beet!

Amy: What kind of nut do you like in your trail mix?

Susy: Cashew.

Amy: Bless you!

Q: What do you get if you throw a microphone in the ocean?

A: A starfish.

Knock, knock.

Who's there?

Annie.

Annie who?

Annie-body else up for a little skydiving today?

Knock, knock.

Who's there?

Tickle.

Tickle who?

A tickle make your dog start itching.

Knock, knock.

Who's there?

Melon.

Melon who?

You're one in a melon!

Q: Why do dragons sleep during the day?

A: They like to fight knights.

Q: How did the snail feel after running a 5K?

A: Sluggish.

Knock, knock.

Who's there?

Feline.

Feline who?

Feline like it's time for an adventure!

Q: What happens when you cross a cow and a comedian?

A: It's udderly ridiculous!

Knock, knock.

Who's there?

Mabel.

Mabel who?

Mabel isn't working, so you'll have to keep knocking.

Q: Why can't chickens play baseball?

A: They hit only fowl balls.

Q: What kind of bird rides in a limo?

A: An ost-rich.

Knock, knock.

Who's there?

Lucas.

Lucas who?

Lucas time to play outside!

Knock, knock.

Who's there?

Raymond.

Raymond who?

Raymond me to wear my helmet when I'm biking.

Q: Why did the math teacher go berry picking?

A: He really liked Pi.

Q: How do you unlock the racing stables?

A: With a joc-key.

Q: What do you get when you cross a fish and a radio?

A: A catchy tuna!

Knock, knock.

Who's there?

Waffle.

Waffle who?

Sorry, the waffle weather made me late!

Laura: My pickles won a blue ribbon at the fair!

Mary: That's a very big dill!

Q: Why did the spider get a job at the computer company?

A: He was a great web designer.

Q: What is a cat's favorite sport?

A: Meow-tain climbing.

Knock, knock.

Who's there?

Douglas.

Douglas who?

Douglas is full of water if you're thirsty.

Knock, knock.

Who's there?

Money.

Money who?

Money is sore from running all day.

Knock, knock.

Who's there?

Alaska.

Alaska who?

Alaska one more time if you can come out and play!

Q: What do fish like best at the playground?

A: The sea-saw.

Q: Why did the dairy farmer cross the road?

A: To get to the udder side.

Knock, knock.

Who's there?

Milton.

Milton who?

Milton snow means no more sledding.

Knock, knock.

Who's there?

Welcome.

Welcome who?

Welcome with you when you go for a ride.

Q: Where do the manatees keep all their money?

A: In the river-bank!

- -

Joe: Why did you put a kazoo in your lunchbox?

Jim: I wanted a hum sandwich!

Q: What kind of mountain can talk?

A: Pikes Speak!

Q: Why did the duck get sent to the principal's office?

A: It was a wise-quacker.

Q: What do a bank and a football game have in common?

A: They both have quarters.

Paul: Do you want to try fencing with me?

Pete: I'll take a stab at it.

Knock, knock.

Who's there?

Canoe.

Canoe who?

Canoe tell me where the paddles are?

Q: Why are turtles always throwing parties?

A: They like to shell-ebrate!

Q: What did the horse do when she fell in love?

A: She got mare-ried.

Q: What do you get if you cross a snail and a camera?

A: Shell-fies.

Q: Why did the rabbit ride the roller coaster?

A: It was looking for a hare-raising experience!

Knock, knock.

Who's there?

Odyssey.

Odyssey who?

Odyssey who's at the door before I answer it.

Q: What do rhinos and credit cards have in common?

A: They both like to charge!

Knock, knock.

Who's there?

Wander.

Wander who?

Wander if we'll go to the ocean this summer.

Q: What do you call a lady who lost all her money?

A: Miss Fortune.

Q: Why couldn't the man get reservations at the restaurant on the moon?

A: It was full.

Q: What did the skunk say after it sprayed the campers?

A: You're so scent-sitive!

Q: Why did the tree go to the beauty shop?

A: It needed to have its roots done.

Q: Why did the boy wear a lampshade for a hat?

A: He felt light-headed.

Q: Where do you find flying rabbits?

A: The hare force.

Q: **What do you call a monster that can really focus?**

A: An aware-wolf.

Q: **When is a plumber like a scuba diver?**

A: When he takes the plunge!

Q: **Why did the fisherman go to the doctor?**

A: He was having trouble with his herring!

Q: **What is a giraffe's favorite fruit?**

A: Neck-tarines!

Knock, knock.

Who's there?

Pasture.

Pasture who?

Pasture house on the way to the park and thought I'd stop by.

Q: What did the chef say after he cooked the steak?

A: Well done!

James: Did you hear the joke about the hot-air balloon?

Jack: It went right over my head!

Knock, knock.

Who's there?

Weasel.

Weasel who?

Weasel be late if you don't open the door!

Q: What do you call a sad dog?

A: A melan-collie.

Q: Why shouldn't you play with a skunk?

A: It's just common scents.

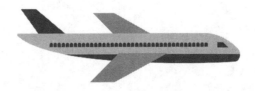

Q: What kind of fruit turns to stone?

A: A pome-granite.

Q: Why don't bakeries let their employees shave?

A: Because they need their whisk-ers.

Q: Where do you buy medicine for your chickens?

A: At the farm-acy.

Q: What did the astronaut take for his headache?

A: A space capsule.

Q: **Why did the train go to the play-ground?**

A: To blow off some steam.

Q: **How do you stay happy when you're running a marathon?**

A: One s-mile at a time!

Q: **What do you do if you catch too many fish?**

A: You scale back!

Q: **What do baseball players eat for dessert?**

A: Bunt (Bundt) cake!

Q: Why won't lobsters laugh at my jokes?

A: Because they're crabby!

Q: What do motorcycle racers eat for lunch?

A: Fast food.

Q: Why did the basketball player throw his banana in the hoop?

A: He wanted to make a fruit basket.

Q: Why do cows go to the gym?

A: To work their calves.

Q: What do night crawlers do before they go for a run?

A: Worm-ups.

Q: What does a basketball player do before she blows out her birthday candles?

A: She makes a swish!

Q: How do you know if you're on a lazy volcano?

A: It's not very active.

Q: What happened when the boy got toilet paper for his birthday?

A: He had a pity potty!

Q: Why did the king go to the dentist?

A: He needed his crown fixed.

Q: What did the mountain say to the valley?

A: You're gorges!

Q: How do you know which flag is the best?

A: You take a pole.

Q: Why did the man dial the canary on the phone?

A: He wanted to try a birdcall.

Q: What does a baker do for fun?

A: Bun-gee jumping!

Q: What happened to the singer after he was hit by lightning?

A: He became a shock star.

Q: Why can't you tell a whale anything?

A: It can't keep a sea-cret.

Q: Why didn't the eagle practice flying?

A: She thought she could just wing it!

Q: How do you get your mom to buy you a kitten?

A: With a little purr-suasion.

Q: What do you call someone with an underwater race car?

A: A scuba driver!

Q: How does it feel if a grizzly steps on your toe?

A: Unbearable!

Tailor: Do you like your new suit?

Customer: It's sew-sew.

Knock, knock.

Who's there?

Candy.

Candy who?

Candy kids come out and play?

Q: Why is bowling like a flat tire?

A: You want a spare.

Q: Why did the spy come out at bed-time?

A: He only works undercovers.

Q: Why don't frogs tell the truth?

A: They're am-fib-ians.

Q: What's a cow's favorite game in gym class?

A: Dodgebull.

Knock, knock.

Who's there?

Waddle.

Waddle who?

Waddle we do when we get to the lake?

Lisa: Why did Mom buy marshmallows?

Leah: She said we needed s'more.

Q: Why did the skier want to go home?

A: He was snow-bored.

Q: How do you buy a map for your trip?

A: You pay the geogra-fee.

Q: What has eighteen wheels and running shoes?

A: A truck and fielder.

Q: Why was the baseball player thirsty?

A: He couldn't find his pitcher.

Q: What do you get when you cross a surfboard and a handkerchief?

A: A boogie board.

Q: Where do baseball players eat their dinner?

A: At home plate.

Trapeze artist #1: Do you like your job at the circus?

Trapeze artist #2: I'm getting into the swing of things.

Q: What do you get when you cross dynamite and a telephone?

A: A boomerang!

Q: What's an astronaut's favorite game?

A: Moon-opoly.

Mom: Do you think it will be a nice hotel?

Dad: I have reservations.

Q: How is Hawaii like your arms?

A: Hawaii has tourists, and your arms have two wrists.

Q: What happened when the river was naughty?

A: It got paddled.

Knock, knock.

Who's there?

Safari.

Safari who?

Safari like this funny joke book!

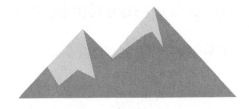

Q: What's the craziest animal in Africa?

A: A hyper-potamus!

Q: What's a frog's favorite game?

A: Croak-et.

Knock, knock.

Who's there?

Atlas.

Atlas who?

Atlas you're answering the door!

Q: Where do pigs like to relax?

A: In a ham-mock.

Q: Why did the horse need a suitcase?

A: It was a globe-trotter.

Q: Where does a peach take a nap?

A: In an apri-cot.

Tammy: Have you heard of the planet Saturn?

Timmy: It has a ring to it.

Lucy: How much is a pair of binoculars?

Lara: I'm looking into it.

Brayden: Have you seen bigfoot?

Hayden: Not yeti!

Jordan: How are your scuba diving lessons going?

Justin: Swimmingly!

Logan: I caught fifty trout with just one worm.

Megan: That sounds a little fishy!

Q: Why did the tuba player go to the nurse?

A: He needed a band-age.

Q: How does a pirate clean his ship?

A: With a treasure mop!

Q: What does a cowboy put on his salad?

A: Ranch dressing.

Q: Why did the gardener put on her dancing shoes?

A: She was going to the hoe-down.

Q: Why do your little brothers always pick on you?

A: It's their expert-tease.

Q: How did the pilot get to the doctor?

A: She flu.

Q: What do you get when you give a rabbit a sleeping bag?

A: A hoppy camper!

Q: Why did the kid's pants fall down in choir?

A: He was belting it out!

Q: When do you bring a hammer on a hike?

A: When you want to hit the trail.

Q: Why did the boy do his homework on a trampoline?

A: So he could get a jump on it.

Andy: There's a skunk in my tent!

Mandy: That stinks.

Q: Why did the diver need a psychiatrist?

A: He was going off the deep end.

Q: What do you get when you cross a tree and chocolate ice cream?

A: A pine cone!

Q: Where do geologists play ball?

A: At the basketball quartz!

Janey: Do you want to look for fossils with me?

Jamie: I dig it!

Knock, knock.

Who's there?

Judah.

Judah who?

Judah thought we'd go on vacation by now.

Q: What kind of poems do you read in the woods?

A: Hike-u.

Q: Why do sea turtles watch the news?

A: To stay up on current events.

Q: How do you keep from losing your telescope?

A: You keep your eye on it.

Knock, knock.

Who's there?

Cashew.

Cashew who?

I'll cashew later.

Knock, knock.

Who's there?

Howdy.

Howdy who?

Howdy come up with this crazy joke?

Knock, knock.

Who's there?

Sherwood.

Sherwood who?

Sherwood be nice to reach our campsite by now.

Harry: My mom won't let me ride the Ferris wheel.

Henry: That's not fair!

Q: How does your grandma give the very best presents?

A: Because she's gifted.

Q: Why did the fish go to jail?

A: Because it was gill-ty.

Knock, knock.

Who's there?

Taylor.

Taylor who?

Taylor it's time to go to the movies.

Q: Why do football players get good grades?

A: They tackle their homework every night.

Q: Why are forest rangers so honest and reliable?

A: It's in their nature.

Q: Why did the astronaut eat steak instead of salad?

A: She wanted something meteor.

Q: Does everybody drink soda?

A: It's pop-ular!

Q: Why are boxers never thirsty?

A: They always beat you to the punch.

Q: How did the secret agent feel when he couldn't crack the code?

A: He was re-Morse-ful.

Jerry: My campsite is better than yours!

Larry: Don't be so pre-tent-ious.

Q: How does it feel to climb a mountain?

A: Ex-hill-arating!

Q: When is a rabbit's foot unlucky?

A: When you're the rabbit.

Q: Why did the astronaut forget his helmet?

A: He was spacey.

Q: Why did the grizzly join the choir?

A: It was a bear-itone.

Knock, knock.

Who's there?

Alto.

Alto who?

Alto the boat to the lake.

Q: How do you play hide-and-seek in the desert?

A: You wear camel-flage.

Q: Why don't we tell jokes about macaroni?

A: They're too cheesy.

Roger: Did you hit my car on purpose?

Roper: No, it was just a coinci-dents.

Q: What happens when your foot falls asleep?

A: It's coma-toes.

Rita: Can you tell me if you brushed your teeth this morning?

Lisa: No, it's confi-dental.

Q: What do you get when you cross a dog and a lobster?

A: A Doberman pincher.

Marney: What happens if bigfoot steps on your toe?

Millie: He'll Sasquatch it.

Knock, knock.

Who's there?

Italy.

Italy who?

Italy a shame if we don't play outside today.

Q: What do you eat underwater?

A: Sub sandwiches.

Q: Why did the kids want to play in the snow?

A: It was ent-icing.

Q: What kind of car does the sun like to drive?

A: An S-UV.

Q: Why did the skunks disappear?

A: They became ex-stinked.

Mandy: My dog brought me a stick all the way from South America.

Mindy: That sounds far-fetched.

Q: What do you call a stinky castle?

A: A fart-ress.

Q: How do you become a conductor?

A: Lots of training!

Q: Why was the astronaut crying?

A: He was a rocket-tear.

Q: What do you eat in a treehouse?

A: A club sandwich.

Q: Did you hear about the giant cow?

A: It's legen-dairy!

Sam: I forgot to pack my bug spray!

Cam: That bites.

Gary: Did you see the movie about the unicorn?

Mary: I'd never myth it!

Q: Where do wasps go on vacation?

A: To the bee-ch.

Q: What did one atom say to the other?

A: You matter.

Q: Why couldn't the skunk make a phone call?

A: It was out of odor.

Q: What did one clown say to the other?

A: You smell funny.

Q: Why did the captain buy a new ship?

A: It was on sail.

Q: What do beavers put on their salads?

A: Branch dressing.

<u>Tongue Twisters:</u>

Mushy marshmallows.

Sort your sport shorts.

Lizards slither.

Slick sticks slip.

Seals steal shells.

Grandpa's cramped camper.

Felines feel fine.

Knock, knock.

Who's there?

Diesel.

Diesel who?

Diesel be the last knock-knock joke in this book!